CHELSEA LEARNS HEBREW

חי

Chelsea Kong

© 2023 Chelsea Kong

All rights reserved. All images used in this book are licensed copies from their respectful owners including myself and Freepik, Pixabay, Pexels, Canva, and Unsplash. This book or any portion thereof may not be reproduced r used in any manner whatsoever without the express written permission of the publisher except for the use of brief quotations in a book review.

Printed in 2023, Made in Toronto, Canada
ISBN: 978-1-990399-26-8
Library and Archives Canada

Hebrew is the main language spoken in Israel.
It is the language of the Jewish people.

You may hear people say "Shalom"
which means "peace."

Hebrew is read from right to left.

There are only 22 letters in the alphabet.
They are consonants and in lower case.

Dotted writing are the letters with added symbols.

There are 9 vowels in the Hebrew alphabet.

We will start with the 22 letters.

The first letter in Hebrew
Alef

ארנב

The second letter in Hebrew
Bet/Vet

אריה

The third letter in Hebrew
Gimel

גימל

ג

The fourth letter in Hebrew
Dalet

דלת
ד

The fifth letter in Hebrew
He

הא

The sixth letter in Hebrew
Vav

ו

The seventh letter in Hebrew
Zayin

ז

ז'ן

The eighth letter in Hebrew
Chet/Knet

Life

חי

חית
ח

The ninth letter in Hebrew
Tet

טית
ט

The tenth letter in Hebrew
Yod

יוד
י

The eleventh letter in Hebrew
Kaf/Khaf

כ ך

כ

The twelfth letter in Hebrew
Lamed

למד

ל

The thirteenth letter in Hebrew
Mem

מם
מ

The fourteenth letter in Hebrew
Nun

נון

נ

The fifteenth letter in Hebrew
Samekh

סמך
ס

The sixteenth letter in Hebrew
Ayin

עין
ע

The seventeenth letter in Hebrew
Pe/Fe

פא
פ

The eighteenth letter in Hebrew
Tzadik/Tsadi

צדי

צ

The nineteenth letter in Hebrew
Kof

קוף
ק

The twentieth letter in Hebrew
Resh

ריש

ר

The twenty-first letter in Hebrew
Shin/Sin

שין
ש

The twenty-second letter in Hebrew
Tav

תו
ת

The first ah vowel in Hebrew
Komatz looks like T but sounds like "ah" in Patach.

The second ah vowel in Hebrew
Patach looks like a flat line and sounds like "ah".

בַ

The third ah vowel in Hebrew Chataf Patach looks like a line and 2 dots is a shorter sound like "ah."

אֲ

The first eh vowel in Hebrew
Segol looks like 3 dots and sounds like "eh" in eggs.

אֶ

The second eh vowel in Hebrew Shva looks like 3 dots (1 on top and 2 on the bottom) and is the short vowel "eh."

The third eh vowel in Hebrew
Chataf Segol looks like 5 dots and sounds like "eh."
It is the smaller vowel.

The first ee vowel in Hebrew
Hirik also called Chirik looks like 1 dot
under the letter and is a long vowel.

אִ

It is like "ee" but sounds like "i" in English.

The second ee vowel in Hebrew
Chirik Malay looks a dot and sounds like "ee" but is like "y" in yogurt.

אִי

The first oh vowel in Hebrew
Cholam Chaser looks a dot above the letter and sounds like a "long o"

אֹ

The second oh vowel in Hebrew Cholam Malay looks like a dot on top of the letter and is a long vowel. It changes v in vav to be "vav"

i

The first oo vowel in Hebrew
Kubutz looks like three dots under the letter and
is a short vowel.

The second oo vowel in Hebrew
Shuruk looks like a dot to the left of the letter
and is a long vowel.

ּו

The second ay vowel in Hebrew Tsere/Tzayray looks like 2 dots under the letter and is a long vowel.

אֵ

Next we will learn important holidays in Hebrew.
These holidays are special.

Blessings come to those who celebrate them.

There are some holidays that are holy to Jews.
There are Christians who like to celebrate too.

Holidays: Purim "Pur פוּר is casting a lot"

Purim פּוּרִים

A celebration of God saving
the Jews from their enemies.

Passover

Pesach חַג הַפֶּסַח
It's a feast and God saved the
first-born sons of the Jews from death.

Feast of Unleavened Bread

Feast of matzah חג המצות / חג המצה / חג הפסח
The feast of eating bread without yeast.
It is the same as the Passover.

Feast of First Fruits

Feast of First Fruits = חג השבועות = חג הבכורים
The time of harvest for the first of everything in the spring time and give God 10%.

Counting the Omer

Sefirat HaOmer סְפִירַת הָעוֹמֶר
Counting the days before Pentecost
and saying the blessing for each day.

Pentecost (50)

Shavuot (Weeks) שָׁבוּעוֹת
The day when the Holy Spirit came on the disciples in the Upper Room.

Feast of Trumpets and Head of the Year

Rosh Hashanah רֹאשׁ הַשָּׁנָה
Yom Teruah יוֹם תְּרוּעָה "day of shouting/blasting"
the shofar to remind God's people
that the Messiah is coming.

New Year

Have a good year.

Day of Atonement/Day of Covering

Yom Kippur יָמִים נוֹרָאִים "Days of Awe"
The high priest gives offering and prayers for God to forgive His people from their sins.

Feast of Tabernacles/Feast of Booths
or Ingathering

Sukkot סֻכּוֹת or סוכות
A feast to wave the lulav and etrog
to get God's blessings for the year.

Sukkot's last day: The Eight Day of Assembly

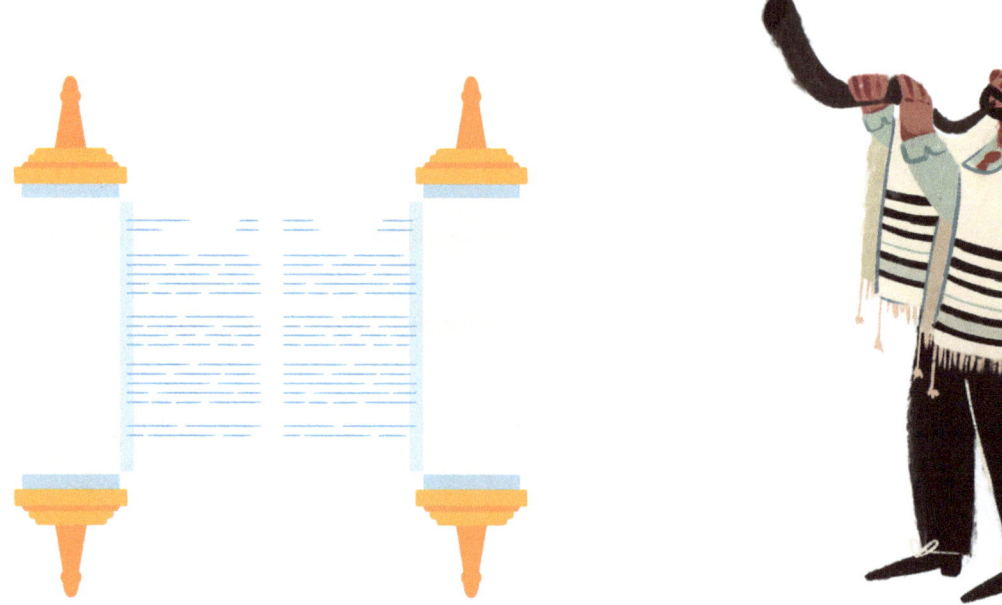

Shemini Atzeret שְׁמִינִי עֲצֶרֶת
The day of Sukkot which is the greatest feast day of celebration.

Festival of Lights/Feast of Dedication

Chanukah/Hanukkah חֲנֻכָּה

Jews light the menorah for 8 days.

Feminine words end with "ה"("h") or "ת"("t"):

- משפחה ("mishpah'a") – family
- מכונית ("meh'onit") – car
- רשימה ("reshima") – list
- אמת ("emet") – truth

Masculine words end with letters other than "ה" or "ת":

- ארץ ("eretz") - country
- אמא ("ima") – mother
- דרך ("dereh' ") - road

Hebrew verbs are usually based on a three ("shoresh" – שורש in Hebrew) letter root
Root: ש-פ-ט ("sh – f/p – t"); י-ד-ע ("y-d-a")

These words are made with the letter root:

- לשפוט ("lishpot") V. – to judge
- לדעת ("ladaat") V – to know something
- שופט ("shofet") V – judge
- ידע ("ye-da") N – knowledge

Hebrew verbs has three tenses.
Root: ש-ח-ק ("s-h'-k")

- The Past (עבר – "avar")
- The Present (הווה – "hove")
- The Future (עתיד – "atid")

Hebrew verbs has three tenses.

Hebrew Past Tense	Hebrew Present Tense	Hebrew Future Tense
הוא שיחק ("hu sih'ek")	הוא משחק ("hu mesah'ek")	הוא ישחק ("hu yesah'ek")
He played	He is playing	He will play

Hebrew adjectives are based on gender.

a big family – (mishpah'a gdola) משפחה גדולה
a big table – ("shulh'an gadokl") שולחן גדול
a good girl – ("yalda tova") ילדה טובה
a good boy – ("yeled tov") ילד טוב

Hebrew sentences has subject, verb, and object.

אני מדברת אנגלית ("ani medaberet anglit")
– I (female) speak English.

אנחנו מבקרים חברים ("anah'nu mevakrim h'averim")
– We are visiting friends.

Vav written has a word written next to it.
An example is "me and you"
אני ואתה

And
- Hebrew: ו...
- Pronounced: ve...

References

Learning Hebrew. LearningHebrew.net, 2012-2013. https://learninghebrew.net/

B'nai Mitzvah Academy. "Hebrew Vowels," B'nai Mitzvah Academy, 2023. https://bnaimitzvahacademy.com/hebrew-vowels-chart/

References

Chabad-Lubavitch Media Center. "The Hebrew Alphabet," Chabad-Lubavitch Media Center, 1993-2023 https://www.chabad.org/library/article_cdo/aid/4069287/jewish/The-Hebrew-Alphabet.htm

References

LinguaJunkie.com.
"Helpful Guide to Hebrew Grammar Rules for Beginners,"
LinguaJunkie.com, 2023
https://www.linguajunkie.com/hebrew/hebrew-grammar-rules

Message from the Author

This book was made to teach the basics of Hebrew in a easy and fun way for children and adults to learn. There are online sources that teach how to pronounce the letters of the alphabets. The most important Jewish hollidays of feasts were added. These special feasts are also in the Bible. Other holidays that Jews celebrate are not known by most people and not as important for people who are interested in the Bible. Rosh Hashannah is also "The Day that Nobody knows."

OTHER PRODUCTS

- Knowing God
- How to Hear God's Voice
- New Life in Jesus
- Loving Israel
- God's Gifts
- Meeting God
- Word Power
- Fruit of the Spirit
- The Tabernacle
- Bride for Jesus
- A Life of Prayer
- Live Free
- Who am I in Jesus
- Walk in Love
- God's Favor
- Man of God
- Woman of God
- How to Use Money
- God's Wisdom
- Fasting
- See Jerusalem and Bethany
- First Fruit Offering
- Feast of Trumpets
- Day of Atonement
- Feast of Tabernacles
- Counting the Omer
- Festival of Lights
- Glory, Presence, and Holy Spirit
- Live in God's Presence
- Pentecost
- See Galilee, Nazareth, and Tiberias
- Hear God Speak
- Knowing Jesus
- Knowing Holy Spirit
- A Healthy Life and Healthy Life Work Book
- Smokey the Cat
- Passover & Unleavened Bread
- Resurrection Life
- The Blessing
- Chelsea's Psalms and Poems
- Revival

OTHER PRODUCTS

Coming soon

Jesus Birth
Loving Jesus: Bride and Groom
Proverbs 31 Woman
Colours in the Bible
Your Daily Meal: Chelsea's Food Album

Devotionals

31 Day Devotional

Puzzle Books

Biblical Puzzle Book Vol 1-5
Bible Puzzles for Young Children Book 1-3
Biblical Puzzle for Children Books 1-5

Teaching Series

How to Hear God's Voice Teaching Guide & Audio Book
Relationship with God, Jesus, Holy Spirit Guide
Knowing God, Jesus, Holy Spirit Guide & Audio Book
Flowing in the Prophetic

Teaching (Non-Sale on my website)
Purim
Passover
Resurrection

More books to come!

BOOK REVIEWS

More books on Amazon, Kobo, and Barnes and Noble, Smashwords
https://chelseak532002550.wordpress.com/

More books on Amazon, Kobo, and Barnes and Noble, Smashwords
https://www.amazon.com/author/chelseakong

Please leave a review and share with friends to help the author continue to write more books to reach more readers. Thank you so much for your support.

Review!

About
CHELSEA KONG

She is a writer, creative arts and digital media artist, skilled administration professional, and podcaster. Chelsea also served in a variety of roles, from audiovisual, photography, to assisting on the worship team, and ministry team. She also has a passion for families being united.

Chelsea has been a guest on Unity Live Radio, The Lady Tracey Show, and How to Live for Christ and is highly recommended by a Proud Christian blog. She is also a guest blogger. A few of her books have been featured in YourAuthorHub, etc. She graduated from Hotel and Restaurant Management, Digital Media Arts, Office Administration, Payroll Professional, and experience working with children. Chelsea lives in Toronto, Canada. She mainly writes children's books, stories, bridal writing, poems, lyrics for songs, words of encouragement, blessings, prayers, and jokes. The author of How to Hear the Voice of God, the Bridal Collection, Knowing God, etc. She also has her own Bible Puzzle books and other inspired products. Her podcast channel is called Chelsea K on Anchor, Spotify, and iTunes.

Please check my website to find out more:
https://chelseak532002550.wordpress.com/

www.ingramcontent.com/pod-product-compliance
Lightning Source LLC
Chambersburg PA
CBHW042006150426
43194CB00003B/143